MARCILLINUS ASOGWA

Voices of Conscience: Stories of Justice Prevailed

First edition

This book was professionally typeset on Reedsy.
Find out more at reedsy.com

Contents

Contents

1

The Enigmatic Inheritance

As the sun dipped below the horizon, casting long shadows across the sprawling estate, the air was thick with anticipation. At the heart of it all stood Sophia Blackwood, the sole heir to the Blackwood fortune. Her pulse quickened as she stood before the imposing doors of Blackwood Manor, a sense of foreboding weighing heavy on her shoulders. Tonight, she would inherit her family's wealth, but little did she know, it would come with a price she never imagined.

The grand doors creaked open, revealing the opulent interior of the manor. Sophia's footsteps echoed through the marble foyer as she made her way towards the center of the room, where a small gathering had assembled. Among them stood her lawyer, Mr. Harrington, his somber expression betraying the gravity of the occasion.

"Miss Blackwood," he began, his voice low and measured, "it is my solemn duty to inform you of the terms of your inheritance." Sophia's heart fluttered nervously as she listened intently, her gaze fixed on Mr. Harrington's every word.

"You are to inherit the entirety of the Blackwood fortune," he continued, "on one condition." Sophia's brow furrowed in confusion, her mind racing to comprehend the implications of his statement.

"What condition?" she pressed, her voice barely above a whisper. Mr. Harrington's eyes bore into hers, a hint of unease flickering behind his steely gaze.

"You must uncover the truth behind your father's death," he declared, his words hanging in the air like a heavy shroud. Sophia's breath caught in her throat as she struggled to process the magnitude of his revelation.

"My father's death?" she repeated, her voice trembling with disbelief. Mr. Harrington nodded solemnly, his expression unreadable.

"Yes," he confirmed, "there are those who believe foul play was involved. You must uncover the truth if you wish to claim your inheritance." With those ominous words, he handed Sophia a small envelope, sealed with the Blackwood family crest.

"Inside you will find the first clue," he explained, "follow it, and it will lead you on the path to uncovering the truth." Sophia's hands shook as she took the envelope, her mind swirling with a whirlwind of emotions.

As the gathering dispersed, leaving Sophia alone in the cavernous foyer, she couldn't shake the feeling of unease that gnawed at her insides. With trembling hands, she tore open the envelope, revealing a single sheet of paper bearing a cryptic message:

"Seek the truth where shadows linger, and secrets lie buried. Trust no one, for danger lurks in the darkness."

Sophia's heart raced as she read the ominous words, a chill creeping up her spine. Little did she know, her journey to uncover the truth would lead her down a perilous path fraught with danger and deception, where the line between friend and foe blurred into obscurity.

2

The Cryptic Warning

The moon hung low in the sky, casting an eerie glow over the deserted streets of the city. Sophia Blackwood sat alone in her dimly lit study, the weight of the inheritance pressing down on her like a suffocating blanket. The cryptic message she had received earlier echoed in her mind, its meaning as elusive as ever.

With a furrowed brow, Sophia stared at the piece of paper clutched tightly in her hand, the words taunting her with their ambiguity. "Trust no one, for danger lurks in the darkness." The warning sent shivers down her spine, a cold dread settling in the pit of her stomach.

Suddenly, a faint rustling sound broke the silence, causing Sophia to startle in her seat. Her heart raced as she scanned the room, her senses on high alert. Could it be her imagination playing tricks on her, or was there someone else in the house?

With trembling hands, Sophia reached for the antique letter opener lying on her desk, her fingers closing around the cold metal with a sense of urgency. Every creak of the floorboards, every whisper of the wind outside, sent a jolt of adrenaline coursing through her veins.

Just as Sophia's nerves reached their breaking point, a soft knock sounded at the door, causing her to jump in her seat. "Who's there?" she called out, her voice barely above a whisper. There was no response, only the sound of her own rapid heartbeat echoing in her ears.

Summoning every ounce of courage she possessed, Sophia rose from her chair and crossed the room, her hand poised to turn the doorknob. With a deep breath, she flung the door open, her eyes scanning the empty hallway beyond.

To her relief, there was nobody there, only the faint glow of the moonlight filtering through the window. Sophia let out a shaky sigh, her shoulders sagging with the weight of her own paranoia. Perhaps she was letting her imagination run wild, allowing fear to cloud her judgment.

But just as she began to convince herself that she was alone, a sudden movement caught her eye, causing her blood to run cold. Across the hallway, a shadowy figure darted out of sight, disappearing into the darkness like a ghost.

Heart pounding in her chest, Sophia's mind raced with a million questions. Who was the mysterious figure lurking in the shadows? And what did they want with her? With a newfound sense of determination, she knew one thing for certain: she couldn't afford to let her guard down, not for a single moment.

As she retreated back into the safety of her study, Sophia resolved to heed the cryptic warning she had received. Trust no one, for danger lurks in the darkness. With that thought weighing heavily on her mind, she knew that her journey to uncover the truth had only just begun. And in a world where secrets lay buried and shadows lingered, she would need every ounce of courage she possessed to survive.

3

Pursued by Shadows

The night air hung heavy with the promise of danger as Sophia Blackwood navigated the dimly lit streets of the city. Every shadow seemed to conceal a lurking threat, every sound sending a shiver down her spine. But she pressed on, driven by an insatiable need to uncover the truth behind her father's death and claim her inheritance.

As she walked, Sophia couldn't shake the feeling of being watched, the hairs on the back of her neck standing on end. She quickened her pace, her footsteps echoing against the pavement as she sought refuge in the anonymity of the crowded streets.

But no matter how fast she walked or how many turns she took, the feeling of being followed persisted, a silent specter haunting her every move. Glancing over her shoulder, Sophia caught a glimpse of a shadowy figure lurking in the darkness, their eyes burning with an intensity that sent a chill down her spine.

Heart pounding in her chest, Sophia broke into a run, her breath coming in ragged gasps as she darted through the labyrinthine streets, her pursuer hot on her heels. Panic surged through her veins as she realized she was being hunted, a pawn in a deadly game she didn't understand.

With every corner she turned, every alley she ducked into, the figure seemed to draw closer, their presence a looming threat that refused to be shaken. Desperation clawed at Sophia's chest as she searched frantically for a way out, her mind racing with a million possibilities.

Just when she thought she couldn't run any farther, Sophia spotted a flicker of light up ahead, a beacon of hope in the darkness. With renewed determination, she sprinted towards it, her lungs burning with exertion as she pushed herself to the brink.

As she burst into the pool of light, Sophia found herself standing before the entrance to an old abandoned warehouse, its towering silhouette looming ominously against the night sky. Without a moment's hesitation, she ducked inside, the heavy door slamming shut behind her with a resounding thud.

Breathless and trembling, Sophia pressed herself against the wall, her heart pounding in her chest as she waited for her pursuer to reveal themselves. But to her surprise, there was only silence, the stillness of the warehouse echoing in her ears like a deafening roar.

For a long moment, Sophia stood frozen in place, her senses on high alert as she scanned the shadows for any sign of movement. But as the minutes ticked by without incident, she began to relax, the tension draining from her body like water from a broken dam.

With a weary sigh, Sophia sank to the ground, her back pressed against the cold concrete floor as she allowed herself a moment of respite. But even as she closed her eyes and let the exhaustion wash over her, she knew that the danger had only just begun. For in a city where shadows concealed secrets and danger lurked around every corner, she couldn't afford to let her guard down, not for a single moment.

4

Betrayal's Bitter Sting

The morning sun cast a golden glow over the city skyline, its warmth a stark contrast to the cold grip of betrayal that tightened around Sophia Blackwood's heart. She sat alone in her study, the events of the previous night replaying in her mind like a cruel joke.

As she stared at the cryptic message lying on her desk, Sophia couldn't shake the feeling of unease that gnawed at her insides. The warning to trust no one echoed in her thoughts, a constant reminder of the dangers that lurked in the shadows.

But even as she grappled with her own fears, Sophia couldn't ignore the nagging suspicion that someone close to her had betrayed her trust. Could it be Mr. Harrington, her father's loyal lawyer, who had delivered the ominous message? Or perhaps it was someone else entirely, someone she had never suspected?

Lost in her thoughts, Sophia barely noticed the soft knock at the door, her heart skipping a beat as she turned to see who it was. To her surprise, it was Mr. Harrington, his expression grave as he entered the room.

"Miss Blackwood," he began, his voice low and measured, "there's something you need to know." Sophia tensed at the seriousness of his tone, her senses on high alert.

"What is it?" she asked, her voice barely above a whisper. Mr. Harrington hesitated for a moment, as if gathering his thoughts.

"I'm afraid I have some troubling news," he confessed, his gaze flickering with guilt. Sophia's heart sank at his words, a sinking feeling settling in the pit of her stomach.

"What kind of news?" she pressed, her voice trembling with apprehension. Mr. Harrington took a deep breath, his expression pained.

"It pains me to say this, but there are those who seek to undermine your claim to the Blackwood fortune," he explained, his words sending a chill down Sophia's spine. "They will stop at nothing to see you fail."

Sophia's mind reeled at the revelation, her thoughts racing with a million possibilities. Who could possibly want to see her fail, and why? And more importantly, how could she possibly hope to overcome such powerful adversaries?

But before she could voice her concerns, Mr. Harrington spoke again, his voice filled with regret.

"I'm afraid I must confess," he admitted, his gaze dropping to the floor, "I have been working with them all along." Sophia's breath caught in her throat at his confession, her world crumbling around her like a house of cards.

"Betrayal's bitter sting," she whispered, her voice barely audible above the pounding of her own heart. In that moment, Sophia knew that she was truly alone, that the trust she had placed in others had been nothing more than a fool's errand.

With a heavy heart, she watched as Mr. Harrington turned to leave, his footsteps echoing in the silence of the room like a death knell. And as the door closed behind him, Sophia was left to confront the harsh reality of her own naivety, knowing that the road ahead would be fraught with danger and deceit.

5

Race Against Shadows

The moon hung low in the night sky, casting eerie shadows across the city streets as Sophia Blackwood darted through the labyrinth of alleyways, her breath coming in ragged gasps. Every step she took was fraught with urgency, every corner turned a gamble with fate.

Behind her, the relentless pursuit continued, the sound of footsteps echoing in her ears like a sinister symphony. With every passing moment, Sophia could feel the danger drawing closer, a shadowy presence that threatened to swallow her whole.

But she couldn't afford to falter, not now, not when the fate of her inheritance hung in the balance. With every ounce of strength she possessed, Sophia pushed herself onward, her mind racing with a single thought: she had to uncover the truth before it was too late.

As she raced through the darkness, Sophia's thoughts turned to the cryptic message she had received, its words burning in her mind like a beacon of hope. "Seek the truth where shadows linger, and secrets lie buried." It was the only clue she had, the only thread connecting her to the elusive truth she so desperately sought.

But even as she clung to the hope of salvation, Sophia couldn't shake the feeling of doubt that gnawed at her insides. Could she really trust the words of a stranger, a voice from the shadows with no name or face to speak of?

With a heavy heart, Sophia pushed the doubts aside, knowing that she had no other choice but to press onward. For in a city where danger lurked around every corner, she couldn't afford to let fear dictate her actions.

As she rounded yet another corner, Sophia stumbled upon a dimly lit alleyway, its narrow passage shrouded in darkness. Without hesitation, she plunged into its depths, her senses on high alert as she scanned the shadows for any sign of danger.

But just as she began to relax, a sudden movement caught her eye, sending a jolt of adrenaline coursing through her veins. Before she could react, a figure emerged from the darkness, their eyes burning with a sinister gleam.

With a cry of alarm, Sophia stumbled backward, her heart pounding in her chest as she realized the danger she was in. But even as she prepared to defend herself, a voice cut through the silence, sending a shiver down her spine.

"Sophia Blackwood," it whispered, its tone dripping with malice, "we meet at last." Sophia's blood ran cold at the sound of the voice, a voice she knew all too well.

With growing horror, she watched as the figure stepped forward, revealing their true identity: none other than her former ally, Mr. Harrington. His lips curled into a cruel smile as he advanced, his eyes gleaming with triumph.

"I must admit, I didn't expect you to make it this far," he taunted, his voice laced with arrogance. "But now that you're here, there's no escaping your fate."

6

The Hidden Chamber of Truth

Sophia Blackwood's heart hammered in her chest as she faced her betrayer, Mr. Harrington, in the dimly lit alleyway. His presence loomed over her like a dark cloud, casting a shadow of fear and uncertainty.

"What do you want from me?" Sophia demanded, her voice trembling with a mixture of anger and fear. Mr. Harrington's smile widened, a glint of malice dancing in his eyes.

"Oh, my dear Sophia," he purred, "I want nothing more than what is rightfully mine." Sophia's brow furrowed in confusion. What could Mr. Harrington possibly want from her that he didn't already have?

Before she could voice her thoughts, Mr. Harrington gestured towards a nondescript door at the end of the alleyway, its weathered surface barely visible in the dim light.

"Inside lies the key to your inheritance," he explained cryptically, his tone dripping with anticipation. Sophia's pulse quickened at his words, her curiosity piqued despite herself.

With cautious steps, Sophia approached the door, her hand trembling as she reached for the handle. With a deep breath, she pushed it open, revealing a narrow staircase descending into darkness.

With Mr. Harrington close behind, Sophia descended into the depths of the unknown, her senses on high alert as she scanned her surroundings for any sign of danger.

As they reached the bottom of the staircase, Sophia found herself standing in a vast chamber, its walls lined with shelves upon shelves of dusty tomes and ancient artifacts. In the center of the room stood a pedestal, upon which sat a small, ornate chest.

With trembling hands, Sophia approached the chest, her heart pounding in her chest as she lifted the lid. Inside, she found a collection of old journals and faded photographs, each one a piece of her family's history.

But as she sifted through the contents, Sophia's eyes fell upon a single photograph that sent a shiver down her spine. It was a picture of her father, standing beside a group of men she didn't recognize, their faces twisted in sinister smiles.

"What is this?" Sophia whispered, her voice barely above a whisper. Mr. Harrington stepped forward, a gleam of triumph in his eyes.

"That, my dear Sophia," he began, "is the truth you've been searching for." Sophia's heart raced as she realized the implications of his words. Could it be that her father's death was not the accident she had always believed it to be?

With trembling hands, Sophia turned to Mr. Harrington, her eyes blazing with determination.

"Tell me everything," she demanded, her voice ringing with authority. Mr.

Harrington's smile faded, replaced by a look of resignation.

"Very well," he sighed, "but know this: once you know the truth, there is no going back."

And with that, he began to recount the events that had led to her father's untimely demise, each word sending a chill down Sophia's spine. As the truth unfurled before her, Sophia realized that her journey was far from over. For in a world where secrets lurked behind every corner, she knew that the path to justice would be fraught with danger and deception.

7

Confrontation in the Shadows

Sophia Blackwood's mind raced with the revelations she had uncovered in the hidden chamber. The truth about her father's death had shattered her perception of reality, leaving her reeling with a sense of betrayal and anger. With resolve burning in her veins, she knew she had to confront those responsible and bring them to justice.

Gathering her courage, Sophia emerged from the chamber, the weight of her newfound knowledge heavy upon her shoulders. The air outside was thick with tension, the city streets cloaked in shadows that seemed to whisper secrets of their own.

As Sophia navigated the labyrinthine alleyways, her senses on high alert, she couldn't shake the feeling of being watched. Every shadow seemed to conceal a lurking threat, every sound sending a shiver down her spine.

But she pressed on, driven by a relentless determination to see justice prevail. With each step, she drew closer to her goal, her heart pounding in anticipation of the confrontation that lay ahead.

Finally, Sophia arrived at her destination: a derelict warehouse on the outskirts of the city, its crumbling facade a stark contrast to the opulence of the Blackwood estate. With a deep breath, she pushed open the creaking door and stepped inside.

The interior of the warehouse was shrouded in darkness, broken only by the faint glow of moonlight filtering through the cracked windows. Sophia's footsteps echoed against the cold concrete floor as she made her way further into the depths of the building, her senses on high alert for any sign of danger.

Suddenly, a voice cut through the silence, sending a chill down Sophia's spine. "Well, well, well, what do we have here?" it taunted, its tone dripping with malice. Sophia spun around to face the source of the voice, her heart racing with a mixture of fear and anger.

Standing before her was Mr. Harrington, his expression twisted into a mocking grin. Beside him stood a group of shadowy figures, their faces obscured by the darkness.

"So, you've come to confront us, have you?" Mr. Harrington sneered, his eyes gleaming with arrogance. Sophia clenched her fists, her jaw set with determination.

"I know the truth now," she declared, her voice steady despite the fear that churned in her stomach. "I know what you did to my father, and I won't rest until you're brought to justice."

Mr. Harrington's laughter echoed through the warehouse, a chilling sound that sent shivers down Sophia's spine. "Justice?" he scoffed. "You think you can bring us to justice? You're nothing but a pawn in our game, Sophia. You always have been."

Sophia's blood boiled at his words, her fists trembling with rage. But before she could respond, Mr. Harrington raised a hand, signaling to his cohorts.

Suddenly, the warehouse was alive with movement as the shadowy figures closed in around Sophia, their intentions clear. With a surge of adrenaline, Sophia prepared to defend herself, knowing that the battle ahead would be her toughest yet.

As fists flew and voices shouted, Sophia fought with all the strength she possessed, her determination unwavering despite the odds stacked against her. In the darkness of the warehouse, surrounded by enemies on all sides, she knew that the fate of her family's legacy hung in the balance. And as she faced her adversaries head-on, she vowed to never back down until justice prevailed.

8

Unveiling the Mastermind

As Sophia Blackwood fought valiantly against her assailants in the dimly lit warehouse, a sense of desperation gnawed at her resolve. With every blow exchanged, she felt the weight of the conspiracy pressing down upon her, threatening to snuff out her determination like a candle in the wind.

But even as the odds seemed stacked against her, Sophia refused to surrender to despair. With each strike, she summoned a reserve of strength she never knew she possessed, her resolve burning brighter with every passing moment.

As the chaos raged around her, Sophia's mind raced with the realization that Mr. Harrington was merely a pawn in a much larger game. If she was to uncover the true mastermind behind her father's death and the conspiracy surrounding her inheritance, she would need to delve deeper into the shadows that concealed their identity.

With a burst of adrenaline, Sophia fought her way through the throng of adversaries, her eyes scanning the darkness for any sign of her elusive quarry. And then, amidst the chaos, she caught a glimpse of movement in the shadows, a figure lurking in the periphery of her vision.

Without hesitation, Sophia pursued the figure, her footsteps echoing against the cold concrete floor as she chased them deeper into the labyrinth of the warehouse. With each step, her determination grew, fueled by a fierce determination to uncover the truth no matter the cost.

Finally, Sophia cornered her prey in a secluded corner of the warehouse, their back pressed against the cold, unforgiving wall. With a sense of triumph coursing through her veins, she stepped forward, her gaze locking with theirs in a silent challenge.

"Who are you?" Sophia demanded, her voice ringing with authority. The figure before her hesitated for a moment, their face obscured by the darkness.

"I am but a servant of a greater power," they replied cryptically, their voice echoing in the silence of the warehouse. Sophia's brow furrowed in confusion. Who could possibly wield such influence over her fate?

Before she could press for answers, the figure stepped forward into the dim light, revealing their true identity: none other than Sophia's estranged uncle, Marcus Blackwood. His eyes gleamed with a mix of cunning and malice, his lips curled into a sinister smile.

"So, we finally meet, dear niece," Marcus sneered, his voice dripping with contempt. Sophia's heart sank at the sight of him, her mind reeling with disbelief. How could her own flesh and blood betray her in such a manner?

With a mixture of anger and sorrow, Sophia confronted her uncle, demanding answers for his treacherous actions. And as Marcus revealed the extent of his involvement in the conspiracy that had plagued her family for years, Sophia realized that the road to justice would be far more treacherous than she ever imagined.

But despite the daunting challenges that lay ahead, Sophia remained steadfast in her resolve. For in the face of betrayal and deceit, she knew that the only path forward was to confront her demons head-on and fight for the truth with every fiber of her being. And with her uncle's true colors finally unveiled, Sophia vowed to stop at nothing to see justice prevail.

9

The Desperate Escape

As Sophia Blackwood confronted her treacherous uncle, Marcus, in the dimly lit warehouse, a sense of urgency gripped her heart like a vice. With each revelation he unveiled, the web of deceit surrounding her family's legacy grew ever more tangled, threatening to consume her whole.

With resolve burning in her veins, Sophia knew she had to escape the clutches of her uncle and his cohorts before it was too late. Every moment spent in their presence increased the risk of falling victim to their nefarious schemes.

Gathering her wits, Sophia feigned compliance, her mind racing with thoughts of strategy and survival. She played the part of the dutiful niece, nodding along with Marcus's sinister plans while biding her time for the perfect opportunity to make her move.

Finally, as Marcus turned his attention to his cronies, Sophia seized her chance. With lightning speed, she darted towards the nearest exit, her heart pounding in her chest with each step. The sound of her footsteps echoed through the cavernous warehouse, a symphony of desperation and determination.

But just as Sophia reached the door, a figure emerged from the shadows, blocking her path with a menacing grin. It was one of Marcus's henchmen, his eyes gleaming with malice as he advanced towards her.

With nowhere left to run, Sophia steeled herself for a confrontation, her fists clenched tight with resolve. She knew that she couldn't afford to show any weakness in the face of her adversary, not if she hoped to escape with her life.

As the henchman lunged towards her, Sophia dodged his attack with lightning reflexes, her movements fueled by a primal instinct for survival. With a swift kick to his midsection, she sent him sprawling to the ground, buying herself precious seconds to flee.

With renewed determination, Sophia raced towards the exit, her heart pounding in her ears as she pushed herself to the limit. Behind her, she could hear the sounds of pursuit, the henchmen hot on her heels as she raced through the darkness.

But Sophia refused to be caught, refused to let her uncle and his cohorts win. With every ounce of strength she possessed, she pushed herself harder, faster, until she could see the light of freedom beckoning from beyond the warehouse doors.

And then, with one final burst of energy, Sophia burst through the exit, her lungs burning with exertion as she stumbled into the cool night air. With a sense of relief washing over her, she raced into the darkness, putting as much distance between herself and her pursuers as possible.

As she ran, Sophia's mind raced with thoughts of what lay ahead. She knew that her escape was only the beginning, that the road to justice would be fraught with peril and uncertainty. But with her freedom secured, she vowed to never give up the fight, to see justice prevail no matter the cost. And with her uncle's sinister plans foiled for now, Sophia knew that the battle for truth was far from over.

10

Forming Alliances

As Sophia Blackwood raced through the labyrinthine streets of the city, her breath coming in ragged gasps, she knew that she couldn't face her enemies alone. With danger lurking around every corner and betrayal lurking in the shadows, she needed allies she could trust.

With a sense of urgency burning in her veins, Sophia sought out those who might be willing to aid her in her quest for justice. She knew that she couldn't rely on her own strength alone if she hoped to uncover the truth and reclaim her family's legacy.

Her first stop was at the doorstep of an old friend, Elijah, a trusted confidant from her childhood. With a sense of trepidation, Sophia knocked on the door, her heart pounding in her chest as she waited for a response.

To her relief, Elijah opened the door, his eyes widening in surprise at the sight of her. "Sophia," he exclaimed, "what are you doing here? Is everything alright?"

Sophia wasted no time in explaining the gravity of the situation, recounting the events that had led to her flight from the warehouse and her desperate need for allies in the fight against her uncle and his cohorts.

Elijah listened intently, his expression growing increasingly grave with each passing moment. "I had no idea things had gotten so dire," he admitted, his voice heavy with concern. "But you can count on me, Sophia. I'll do whatever it takes to help you."

With Elijah's support secured, Sophia knew that she had taken the first step towards forming the alliances she needed to see justice prevail. But she also knew that she couldn't stop there.

Her next stop was at the doorstep of another old friend, Maria, a skilled hacker with a knack for uncovering secrets hidden in the digital realm. With a sense of determination burning in her chest, Sophia sought out Maria's expertise in navigating the treacherous waters of cyberspace.

When Maria opened the door, she greeted Sophia with a warm smile, her eyes sparkling with curiosity. "Sophia, what brings you here?" she asked, her tone tinged with anticipation.

Sophia wasted no time in explaining the danger she was facing and her desperate need for someone with Maria's skills to help her uncover the truth. Maria listened intently, her expression growing increasingly serious as Sophia recounted the events that had led her to seek refuge in her friend's home.

After a moment of contemplation, Maria nodded solemnly. "You can count on me, Sophia," she declared, her voice filled with determination. "I'll do whatever it takes to help you bring those responsible to justice."

With Maria's expertise in her corner, Sophia knew that she had taken another crucial step towards unraveling the conspiracy that had plagued her family for so long. But as she looked towards the uncertain future that lay ahead, she knew that the battle for truth was far from over. With her allies by her side, Sophia vowed to press forward, no matter the cost, until justice prevailed. And with the support of those she trusted most, she knew that nothing could stand in her way.

11

Unraveling the Conspiracy

With Elijah and Maria at her side, Sophia Blackwood felt a renewed sense of determination coursing through her veins. Together, they formed a formidable team, each bringing their own unique skills to the table in the fight against the conspiracy that had plagued her family for generations.

As they gathered in Elijah's dimly lit living room, Sophia outlined their plan of attack, her voice steady despite the weight of uncertainty that hung in the air. With each passing moment, the walls seemed to close in around them, the sense of danger palpable.

Their first task was to uncover the extent of Marcus Blackwood's involvement in the conspiracy, and to do that, they needed access to information that had long been kept hidden from view. With Maria's expertise in hacking, they set out to penetrate the digital defenses that guarded their family's darkest secrets.

As Maria worked her magic on the keyboard, her fingers flying across the keys with lightning speed, Sophia and Elijah stood watch, their senses on high alert for any sign of danger. With each passing moment, the tension in the room grew, the anticipation of what they might uncover hanging heavy in the air.

And then, just as they began to lose hope, Maria's face lit up with triumph. "I've found it," she declared, her voice ringing with excitement. "The key to unlocking the truth."

With bated breath, Sophia and Elijah gathered around the computer screen, their eyes scanning the lines of code that revealed the hidden depths of the conspiracy that had torn their family apart. As they delved deeper into the digital labyrinth, they uncovered a web of deceit that stretched far beyond anything they had ever imagined.

But their triumph was short-lived, for even as they uncovered the truth, danger lurked around every corner. With a sense of urgency burning in their hearts, they knew that they had to act fast if they hoped to outmaneuver their adversaries and bring them to justice.

Their next task was to confront Marcus Blackwood himself, to expose his treachery and put an end to his reign of terror once and for all. With a plan in place, they set out into the night, the shadows concealing their movements as they made their way towards their final confrontation.

As they approached Marcus's sprawling estate, a sense of foreboding settled over them like a heavy cloak. With each step, the weight of their mission pressed down upon them, the knowledge that their lives hung in the balance fueling their determination to see justice prevail.

Finally, they reached the imposing gates of the estate, their hearts pounding in their chests as they prepared to face their greatest adversary. With a deep breath, Sophia pushed open the gates, her eyes blazing with determination as she stepped into the lion's den.

But as they entered the estate grounds, they were met with an unexpected sight: Marcus Blackwood, standing before them with a sinister smile on his lips. "So, you've come to confront me at last," he sneered, his voice dripping with malice. "How predictable."

With a sense of dread settling in the pit of her stomach, Sophia knew that their final confrontation would be their most dangerous yet. But with Elijah and Maria at her side, she knew that she had the strength and courage to face whatever lay ahead. And as they stood together in the face of adversity, they knew that no matter the outcome, they would fight until the bitter end to see justice prevail.

12

The Final Showdown

As Sophia Blackwood, Elijah, and Maria stood before Marcus Blackwood in the imposing grounds of his estate, a tense silence settled over them like a shroud. The air crackled with anticipation, each breath heavy with the weight of the impending confrontation.

Marcus regarded them with a cold, calculating gaze, his lips curled into a twisted smile. "Well, well, well," he sneered, his voice dripping with malice. "It seems you've stumbled into the lion's den, my dear niece. But you won't find safety here."

Sophia met his gaze with steely determination, her jaw set in a defiant line. "We're not here for safety," she declared, her voice ringing with authority. "We're here for the truth, Marcus. And we won't rest until justice is served."

Marcus's smile faltered for a moment, a flicker of uncertainty crossing his features before being replaced by a mask of icy composure. "Justice?" he scoffed. "You speak of justice as if it's something you can attain. But you're just a pawn in a much larger game, Sophia. And in this game, there are no winners, only survivors."

With a wave of his hand, Marcus signaled to his henchmen, who emerged from the shadows with menacing grins. "Take them," he commanded, his voice echoing through the night like a death knell.

With a surge of adrenaline, Sophia, Elijah, and Maria sprang into action, their movements swift and decisive as they faced off against their adversaries. Fists flew and shouts rang out, the sound of the struggle echoing through the estate grounds like thunder.

But despite their determination, Sophia and her allies soon found themselves outnumbered and outmatched. With each passing moment, the odds seemed to stack higher against them, the weight of their enemies pressing down upon them like a suffocating blanket.

Just when it seemed as though all hope was lost, a sudden explosion rocked the estate, sending shockwaves rippling through the air. With a cry of alarm, Marcus's henchmen faltered, their attention momentarily diverted by the chaos unfolding around them.

Seizing the opportunity, Sophia and her allies fought their way through the fray, their movements fueled by a fierce determination to escape the clutches of their enemies. With every step, they drew closer to freedom, their hearts pounding in their chests with each beat.

But just as they reached the safety of the estate gates, they were met with one final obstacle: Marcus Blackwood himself, his eyes burning with fury as he blocked their path.

"You think you can escape me?" he growled, his voice low and menacing. "You may have won this battle, but the war is far from over. I will hunt you to the ends of the earth if I have to, Sophia. You will never be safe from me."

With a defiant glare, Sophia met his gaze head-on, her chin held high in defiance. "We'll see about that," she declared, her voice ringing with determination. "Because as long as we stand together, justice will prevail. And no amount of threats or intimidation will ever change that."

With one final push, Sophia, Elijah, and Maria burst through the gates of the estate, leaving Marcus Blackwood and his henchmen behind in their wake. As they disappeared into the night, a sense of relief washed over them, their spirits buoyed by the knowledge that they had faced their greatest challenge and emerged victorious.

But even as they left the estate grounds behind them, they knew that the battle for truth was far from over. With Marcus Blackwood still at large and the conspiracy that had plagued her family for generations still lurking in the shadows, Sophia knew that their journey was far from over. But with her allies by her side and her resolve stronger than ever, she was ready to face whatever challenges lay ahead. And as they disappeared into the darkness of the night, Sophia knew that no matter what trials awaited them, they would face them together, united in their quest for justice.

Milton Keynes UK
Ingram Content Group UK Ltd.
UKHW022037290324
440241UK00014B/562